How I Began Defending The KJB & Its Underlying Hebrew, Aramaic, & Greek

Bible For Today Baptist Church

Pastor D. A. Waite, Th.D., Ph.D.

THE BIBLE FOR TODAY PRESS
900 PARK AVENUE
COLLINGSWOOD, NEW JERSY 08108
U.S.A.

CHURCH PHONE:856-854-4747
BFT PHONE:856-854-4452
ORDERS: 1-800-JOHN 10:9
BFT@BibleForToday.org
www.BibleForToday.org
fax: 856-854-2464

We Use and Defend
the King James Bible

July, 2020

ISBN: 978-1-7351454-3-3

Publishing assisted by:
The Old Paths Publications, Inc.
www.theoldpathspublications.com
TOP@theoldpathspublications.com

How I Began Defending The KJB & Its Underlying Hebrew, Aramaic, & Greek

By
Pastor D. A. Waite, Th.D., Ph.D.
June 29, 2020

(BFT #4207)

"*For ever, O Lord, Thy Word is settled in Heaven*"
(Psalm 119:89)

I. My Early Days

I was born on December 8,1927, in Elyria, Ohio, to Virgil and Helen Waite. Virgil was a skilled and prosperous Chemical Engineer with the McGean Chemical Company in Cleveland, Ohio. He was a graduate of the University of Michigan with a major in Chemical Engineering. While I was in kindergarten, we moved to Berea, Ohio. My sister, Dorothy, was born two years before me in Elyria, Ohio. My younger sister, Ann, was born about six years afterwards in Berea, Ohio. Grandpa Stanley Waite was a member of the Board of Elections in Elyria, Ohio, and Grandpa Albert Peirce was a roofer in Wellington, Ohio, and also active in the Salvation Army there.

II. The Berea, Ohio, High School

A. Meeting The High School Janitor "Uncle Charley" Allen

I attended kindergarten, elementary school and high school in Ohio. One day, in Berea High School, three of us seniors were eating our lunch in the music room on the first floor. During lunch one day, I went out into the hall to get a drink. We had been talking about creation and how the world came into being. When I went out into the hall, the janitor was sweeping the floor. His name was Mr. Charles Allen, but everyone called him "Uncle Charlie." So I asked him about what we three were talking about. I asked him, "Uncle Charlie, how did the world and all the stars get here?"He looked down at me, smiled, and replied in just two words to me: "I know."

B. Becoming A Genuine Christian

When this Christian janitor had the answer to my question, I thought I would go down to the school boiler room to Uncle Charlie's office, and find out some other things he knew about. He told me in detail how God created the Heaven, the earth, and all the stars.He also told me, for the first time I had ever heard it, the verses from the Gospel of John.

John 3:14-16 "*And as Moses lifted up the serpent in the wilderness, even so must the Son of man be lifted up: That whosoever believeth in him should not perish, but have eternal life. For God so loved the world that He gave His only begotten Son, that whosoever believeth in Him should not perish, but have everlasting life.*"

I believed these verses and trusted the Lord Jesus Christ as my Saviour. Uncle Charlie continued to teach me more about the Bible and its important doctrines. He gave me a leather-bound King James Bible so I could read it and learn more about God's truths.

C. Meeting My Wife-To-Be

When I received the Bible from Uncle Charlie, I took it to my locker to put it away. While I was putting it away, Yvonne Sanborn was at her locker a short distance from mine. She saw me putting my Bible into my locker and asked, "*Where did you get that Bible*?"I told her: "*Uncle Charlie gave it to me. I am his first.*" (meaning the first person he had ever led to Christ). She knew that Uncle Charlie was a genuine Christian, so she asked, "Are you born again and saved?" I said "Yes, I am." From that day, we began to go with one another. . . dating, walking down the aisle together at graduation, and in other ways. She invited me to her mother's weekly Bible classes for young people held in her home. Yvonne also invited me to attend her Bible-believing Berea Baptist Church where I became a regular member from that time forward.

III. Leaving Berea, Ohio

A. Attending The University Of Michigan At Ann Arbor

My Dad was a graduate of the University of Michigan with a Chemical Engineering degree. He thought it would be good for me to be trained at that University where he was trained, so he sent me there. Since I wanted to marry Yvonne Sanborn as soon as possible and since she was planning to attend the Moody Bible Institute in Chicago, Illinois, which would last three years, I decided to take my four years of study at the University of Michigan in three years so we could begin our 71 years of marriage together as soon as possible. So, I was a student at the University of Michigan for 3 years during the Fall, Spring, and Summer, from 1945 to 1948. Upon graduation, I received a Bachelor of Arts degree In Classical Greek and Latin. I was married to Yvonne Sanborn on August 27, 1948.

B. Why Did I Change My Major?

When I went to this University, I was intending to train to be a medical doctor. This changed, however. I was walking along the main street on the University's campus when I noticed a woman who was having trouble with her car. She was out in front of the car with the hood up. All of a sudden, the car started to move forward, pushing her to the ground, causing her to bleed profusely. I was now only a freshmen in the University and only 16 or 17 years of age. Since I was training to become a Medical Doctor, I would have to deal with various kinds of accidents, many of which would deal with such profuse bleeding. It made me afraid of that kind of a future. In fact, I couldn't sleep very well for several nights. The change came when I accepted the call of the Lord to prepare to become a full-time servant of the Lord Jesus Christ instead of becoming a medical doctor.

C. What Had To Be Changed Because Of This Decision?

I needed to change my courses from the preparation for medical school to the preparation for a Theological Seminary. The Chef at the University hospital, Mr. David McRoberts, took me and several other students to attend Dr. M. R. DeHaan's Friday night Bible Classes in the book of Hebrews at Detroit, Michigan. These classes re-enforced my call to prepare to be a Biblical Pastor. I asked Dr. DeHaan what seminary he would recommend that I should attend to best prepare me to be a Bible-trained Pastor. At that time, he would recommend Dallas Theological Seminary where Dr. Lewis Sperry Chafer was the Founder and President. So I applied to that school and began attending. When I told my father, (who was a very prosperous Chemical Engineer) of my change in future plans, he had just one comment: *"From pennies to peanuts in just one generation*!!" He could have stopped providing for this very expensive four years in three, but he didn't. He never fought with me over this choice, but continued to help his only son to prepare for that to which he had been called by the Lord. In fact, when our Baptist Pastor, Pastor Powers Payton, visited Dad in the hospital, near his death, he told him the gospel, and Dad accepted the Lord Jesus Christ as his Saviour. He told that to me when the Pastor left his room. So Dad received something that "pennies" cannot buy.

IV. Attending Dallas Theological Seminary

A. Moving To Dallas, And Receiving My Master Of Theology (Th.M.) Degree, And Doctor Of Theology (Th.D.) Degree

After our marriage, August 27, 1948, my wife and I immediately left Berea, Ohio, and drove down to Dallas, Texas, arriving in September of 1948. We drove in a car that my Dad graciously provided for us. Dad also gave us a beautiful brand-new 26-foot Vagabond house trailer where we lived while in Dallas. During the first four years, I studied two years of Hebrew and four years of Greek. I completed my Master of Theology Degree (Th.M.) with a major in New Testament Greek. The only Greek taught and defended at Dallas Theological Seminary was the false Gnostic text of Bishop Westcott and Professor Hort. In this Greek text are many, many false doctrinal words. I didn't find the true Traditional Greek Text on which the King James Bible is based for almost the next twenty years. During the next two years, I completed the residency courses for my Doctor of Theology (Th.D.) degree with a major in New Testament Greek. Then, later on, I completed my Doctoral dissertation.

B. While At Dallas, I Was Asked To Be A Pastor At A Small Spanish Baptist Church In Dallas

The preparation in learning Spanish was very useful for me to be a Spanish Pastor in this small church under the First Baptist Church of Dallas. I had taken two years of Spanish in High School, and another two years of Spanish at the University of Michigan. Years later, I used this Spanish while flying on an airplane from Philadelphia to Florida. The plane was hijacked. The hijackers forced the pilots to fly the plane to Cuba instead of Florida. The passengers were asked by an airline attendant if anyone on the plane could speak Spanish. I volunteered, and communicated with the passen-gers about what was going to happen. The hijackers were going to keep the people they wanted in Cuba, and send the rest of us back to the USA.

C. My Working At A Factory At A Large Machine

This helped with various expenses while going to Dallas Theological Seminary. I worked at a large machine that made steel equipment for cotton gins. I could memorize my Greek materials while watching this huge machine work.

V. Getting My Master's Degree (M.A.) In Speech

While completing my Doctor of Theology dissertation, we lived for several years in our trailer at Dallas Theological Seminary. While there, I attended Southern Methodist University In Dallas. While a graduate student there, I completed my Master of Arts (M.A.) in Speech. Our first two children,

Don, Jr. and Dave were born there in Dallas.

VI. We Then Moved To Purdue University In Lafayette, Indiana

I began working on my Doctor of Philosophy (Ph.D.) in Speech. Purdue University hired me as a full time Graduate Teaching-Assistant In Speech. As I worked on my Doctor of Philosophy (Ph.D.) degree in Speech, I taught first year classes in Speech. This worked out well for our family because I was paid for teaching, but did not have to pay any college tuition while I worked on my degree. We had a total of five children. Here are the names of our other three children: Dick was born in Ohio, Dianne was born in Florida, and Dan was born in New Jersey.

VII. I Joined The U. S. Navy As A Navy Chaplain

A. I Wanted To Serve My Country, So I Joined The Navy

I was sent to Chaplain's School. Since I graduated first in my class, I was given my choice of my first duty station. I served the Lord as Navy Chaplain at the Marine Corps Air Station, OpaLocka, Florida, near Miami. Both my parents and my wife's parents lived in Florida at that time. After a few months of Chaplains' service in Florida, I was given orders to go for Chaplain duty with the land-based Marines overseas in Okinawa. I was in service there for 10 months without my family who remained in the Miami area.

B. Completing My Naval Chaplaincy Service

I completed my Navy Chaplain's ministry at the Marine Corps Air Station preaching at the Chapel and ministering to the marines and naval personnel. The senior chaplain didn't like my Bible-centered preaching. He said it was boring, stupid, and unnecessary. So, I began another morning service in a different place with his approval. That service drew many more navy and marine people-- even more than came to the regular morning services! The senior chaplain saw what was happening, and wanted to have other Chaplains taking part in my services every other week. But, since I didn't want apostate Chaplains being part of my services, I quit the work that I had begun.

VIII. Teaching Greek And Speech At Shelton College, Cape May, New Jersey

A. Every Tuesday And Thursday, I Taught At This Small School

This small school, which was organized and run by Dr. Carl McIntire, was about 90 miles from my Collingswood home. I drove from Collingswood. N.J. to Cape May each week to teach these classes.

B. It Was While Teaching Greek At Shelton College That I First Heard Of the False And True New Testament Greek Words

I first learned, at this school, that there was in existence a profound refutation of the false Westcott and Hort Greek New Testament words. These false words are those that that underlie nearly all modern New Testaments. It was during one of my regular Greek classes at Shelton College. During one of the classes, one of my young lady students, named Sandra Phillips, raised her hand, and said:

> "*Dr. Waite, I was visiting Princeton University the other day, and found some books written by Dean John William Burgon that refuted the Greek Text that underlies the Revised Version New Testament and many other New Testament modern Bible versions.*"

I thanked Sandy for telling me about this. I had never heard about this before. I was interested very much to learn more about this subject.

IX. My Trip To Princeton University Seminary, In Princeton, New Jersey

A. I left For Princeton As Soon As I Could In Order To See Dean Burgon's Five Books That Sandy Phillips Had Told Me About

When I arrived at the Seminary library, I found all five books written by Dean John William Burgon:
   (1) *The Revision Revised*
   (2) *The Last Twelve Verses of Mark*
   (3) *The Traditional Text Of The Holy Gospels Vindicated*
   (4) *The Causes of Corruption Of the Traditional Text*
   (5) *Inspiration And Interpretation Of The Bible*
I asked the librarian if I could check out all five books and take them home to Collingswood, New Jersey. He said that I could take them out all right.

B. When I Got Home To Collingswood, I Examined Dean Burgon's Five Books

I could see how valuable and scholarly these Dean Burgon books were, so I checked them out and took them home. I saw how they could be used in this battle for the true Bible. I examined all five of these books. I found them unique, scholarly, and useful to others as well. So, I copied them on my copy machine and printed them out so that others might be able to defend the Traditional Greek Words underlying the King James Bible. Dean Burgon stood firmly against Bishop Westcott's and Professor Hort's false Words used in all their doctrinal changes that they believed in. Dean Burgon was chastised for it, because he stood firmly in favor of the Traditional Greek Words that underlie the King

James Bible, rather than the error-filled false words of Westcott and Hort that they had introduced into the Greek that underlies the Revised Version and many other modern Bible versions.

C. When I Looked In My Voluminous BFT Catalog, I Found 40 Articles By Or About Dean John William Burgon

Among the 40 titles, there were not only articles that I had written about Dean Burgon, but there were also many audio tapes about him that I or others had spoken about him and his writings over the radio on many occasions. These are all listed on page 1 of our 89-page *Bible For Today Catalog*. If you wish to see this page 1 of my 89-page catalog of materials, either email me (*BFT@BibleForToday.org,*) or call me at 856-261-9018,or I can FAX a copy page #1 to you.

D. To Make These Books Available To Those Who Wanted Them, I Copied Them On My Copy Machine And Bound Them

I checked out Dean Burgon's five books, and made copies of all of them. Since they were all out of print, and are very much needed, the Bible For Today had them printed in book form so all could buy them, read them, and see the excellent refutation of Westcott and Hort's serious errors regarding their changes in the Greek Words underlying the King James Bible.

X. Recognizing The Need For The Defense Of, And The Integrity Of, The King James Bible, And Its Underlying Greek Words, We Had These Five Books Commercially Printed

A. Here Are The Details On The Cost Of Purchasing These Five Excellent Dean Burgon Books

(1) *The Revision Revised*; BFT#611; 640pp;$25.00+Shipping

(2) *The Last Twelve Verses of Mark*; BFT#1139;400pp;$15.00+Shipping

(3) *The Traditional Text Of The Holy Gospels Vindicated*; BFT#1159; 350pp;$15.00+Shipping

(4) *The Causes of Corruption of the Traditional Text;* BFT#1160; 316pp;$14.00+Shipping

(5) *Inspiration And Interpretation Of The Bible* BFT#1220;567pp; $25.00+Shipping

B. Here's How To Order

Write:

The Bible For Today
900 Park Avenue
Collingswood, New Jersey 08108

Give Us You're your Credit Card
Number, Or Make Your Check Payable
To:

The Bible For Today Baptist Church

Our phone number, if you want to Call
In Your Order, is 856-261-9018

XI. Conclusions

For over 21 years, as Pastor of the Bible For Today Baptist Church in Collingswood, New Jersey, and as the President of the Dean Burgon Society from its founding, I have stood firmly in defense of the King James Bible and its underlying Hebrew, Aramaic, and Greek Words.

This background information has been a very brief summary of how the Lord prepared and led me through this battle for His Name and His Words. He has given me the strength, understanding, and courage to fight for the Authorized King James Bible, and its proper underlying Hebrew, Aramaic, and Greek Words.

I have been surrounded by many, many people who have strong opposition to the truth about the proper Hebrew and Aramaic Old New Testament Words and the Greek New

Testament Words. They rather promote the false Old and New Testament Words that are used as the foundation for the various and erroneous Old and New Testaments now in print all over the world.

By relying on these false Old and New Testaments with their false Hebrew, Aramaic, and Greek words, many perverted doctrines are taught and promoted.

I, for one, had been taught the erroneous views on the Bible and its underlying Hebrew, Aramaic, and Greek Words in many of my classes in school. For this reason, I composed this booklet to urge the readers to (1) get the 5 books by Dean Burgon mentioned in this booklet, (2) study these books carefully, and (3) tell your friends about the importance of these books.

I have made it one of my goals to search out, with God's help and guidance, the truth about the genuine Hebrew, Aramaic, and Greek Words that SHOULD underlie our Old and New Testament Bibles, and expose he FALSE words that now underlie 99% of the Bibles (with the exception of the 1611 King James Bible. This is a vitally important and eternal matter. God has greatly helped me in this goal, and I thank Him for it.

Now, at 92 years of age, the Lord has continued to give me the strength to be faithful to the fight in the battle for the truth of His Words.

BFT #4207

Suggested and Recommended Reading By Pastor D. A. Waite, Th.D., Ph.D.

Here are a few books that I wrote which might be of help in this entire controversy.

1. *Defending the King James Bible;* BFT #1594; 327 pp; $12.00+Shipping

2. *Summary of Burgon's Traditional Text of the Holy Gospels*; BFT #2771; 30 pp;$4.00+Shipping
3. *Summary of Burgon's Causes of Corruption*; BFT#2780; $4.00 +Shipping.
4. *Summary of Burgon's Inspiration and & Interpretation*; BFT#2925;46pp; $4.00+ Shipping.